THUNDER AND LIGHTNING

Poems on African-American Life and Love

Esmo Woods

Fourth printing, 2001

Published by
The New Pontiac History Group
P.O. Box 430063
Pontiac, MI 48343

ISBN 0-9641636-1-6

All rights reserved.

No part of this book may be reproduced in any form or by any electronic or mechanical means, including information storage and retreival systems or photocopy,without the written permission of the publisher, except by a reviewer who may quote brief passages in a review.

Manufactured in the United States of America.

This volume of poems
is dedicated to the
memory of the late
John Coltrane,
African-American
Saxophonist Extraordinaire.

Acknowledgements

There have been many persons who have played some role in the development of this book of poems. Space limitations will only allow for the recognition of a few, although I wish to thank all of those persons who have made contributions to this book of poems in some form or fashion. Special thanks to internationally famous percussionist Elvin Jones for the foreword which he wrote to this book of poems.
    I wish to express my thanks and gratitude to La Chelle McDonald, an alumnus of Pratt Institute in New York, for the sketches which appear in this book; her portrayals of some of the great African American Jazz musicians are much appreciated. I have Walt Thomason to thank for the photograph that accompanies the poem, "With this Ring." I would like to express my deep appreciation to Karen Barner of Pontiac, Michigan, for her unfailing secretarial and computer services. Beth Moss of Butler Graphics is to be thanked for her assistance with layout and design. Though the author appreciates the help and assistance of all of the persons who have made contributions to this work, I am alone responsible for any errors which might appear in the book.

Foreword

This volume of poetry is the odyssey of Esmo Woods. He reveals the most intimate portions of his life, his love of family, his passionate regard for his friends and his unwavering and unshakable integrity. This work evoked in me the works of Langston Hughes, Paul Laurence Dunbar, Richard Wright and E.E. Cummings. Typical of his modest nature, there are no references to his being one of, if not the, greatest basketball players in U.S. history ever.

Though I am not a writer, I am deeply moved and flattered beyond measure to have been asked to write this brief foreword to this labor of love and work of art. In it are the dreams and aspirations of all people.

> Elvin Jones
> The Elvin Jones Jazz Machine
> October 5, 1993

Table of Contents

	Page
CHILDHOOD	
Will someone please come out to play?	1
A Kiss for my neighbor Martha Lee	2
Part I Mother to Son	3
Part II Mother to Son	4
Tall shadows, small shadows	5
Summer Voices	6
Childhood Memories	7
Love After World War II	9
NATURE CALLING	
The Robin's Song	11
Love Calling	11
Transitions	12
Butterflies	13
Morning	14
What Kind of Wind are You	15
WITH LOVING TOUCHES	
For Sandra: One Red Rose	17
A Sweeter Truth: Valentine's Day 1985	18
Promises	19
What if...	20
With This Ring	21
Before You (A Love Poem from the Sixties)	22
Love	23
Lover	24
Promised Land	25
We are the Newlyweds	27
This jewel sipping sweet rum	28
Two in One	29
Prisoner in your Arms	30
No need for bitter memories from the past	31
A poem for Mother Lillian	32
Poem for Hatchett's Baby	33
Shipwrecked	34
Chicago Weekend	35
THE JAZZ IN US	
Toward a dance hall we go	37
Waltzing in the Snow	38
Elvin Jones	39
I saw John	41
Spring	42
Jazz Lovers	43
The Music of the Four Seasons	45
Jazz	46
Songs from the Stormy Sky	47
Part I - Tribute to Trane	
Part II - Tributes from the Living	
Blues Ooze into the Midnight Air	48
Remembering Monk and "Ruby, My Dear"	49

Page

SOCIAL COMMENTS
Pappa's Dream ... 51
Hear That Lonesome Train Whistle ... 52
Inheritance ... 53
Rude Awakening ... 54
The Sale of a Southern Farm ... 55
Electronic Salvation ... 56
The Sweetest Faces on the Earth ... 57
Stars in Heaven Stay in Shape ... 58
Scream Out Loud ... 60
Poem to my Grandmother I Never Saw ... 61

THE LITERARY FIGURES
Of Charles Spurgeon Johnson ... 63
Arna Bontemps ... 64
To Paul Laurence Dunbar's House We Go ... 65
Remembering Robert Hayden ... 66
Purple River ... 67
Robert Hayden, I Didn't Know Who You Were ... 68
A Salute to Nikki Giovanni ... 69

SOCIAL PROTEST
Run, Slaves, Run ... 71
Du Bois ... 72
The Life and Death of a Slave ... 73
A Wily Slave will Always Find a Way ... 75
Legacy of Love ... 77
At Heaven's Golden Podium ... 78
King's Dream ... 79
"Out" ... 80
A Poem for Two Champions of the Cause ... 81
This Land Belongs to All of Us ... 82

FAITH AND HOPE
Words in My Head ... 84
No One Comes to my House, Anymore ... 85
Lord, I'll Confess ... 86
Hear Those Shaking Tambourines ... 87

IN MEMORIUM
My Sister Grows Older Day by Day ... 89
Lines to a Young Hero ... 90
To Mother Kay, Our Distinguished Medal of Honor ... 91
The Farm in Tennessee ... 92
To DeWalt, A Man with a Heart of Gold ... 93
Plato ... 94
Beth ... 95

vii

CHILDHOOD

WILL SOMEONE PLEASE COME OUT TO PLAY?

Will someone please come out to play?
The rain is gone for the day,
I want to hop and skip and run,
I want to play some games for fun,
Too soon we'll all grow up
And move away,
Will someone please come out to play?

1985

A KISS FOR MY NEIGHBOR MARTHA LEE

The teacher kept you after school,
My Neighbor, Martha Lee,
I was fresh from band, playing
"Dancing in the Dark."
When I caught up to you
We walked and talked in the sun
Smiling in each other's eyes;
Something in our heads said
Kiss in broad daylight-
So enthralled by your lips
The strap to my drum
Fell off my shoulder to the ground;
Snares made a rattling sound,
Like a snake in the grass;
We quickly looked around
But nobody saw us,
So we resumed our homeward jaunt
Laughing to beat the band.

1987

PART I MOTHER TO SON

Dinner is almost ready, son
The mother called to him
But we need a package of orange Kool-Aid
Wipe that look off your face
Button up your overcoat
Put your hand to your mouth when you cough
Take this spoonful of castor oil
Stop making those faces
Wipe your feet at the door
Bow your head for the blessing
Go do your homework
Don't forget to bank the fire
And don't forget to say your prayers
Stop clowning in there
Cut out all the noise
Go to sleep, it's late
Get up, you'll be late for school
Here's your lunch money
Straighten out your shirt collar
Do your best in school, son,
I'm so proud of you.

PART II MOTHER TO SON

"Momma" the son said,
"When I grow bigger,
I'm going to buy for you
A big house, Momma,
A big car, Momma,
And a big, —"
"Listen Sonny, listen good,"
His mother said to him,
"Momma's not young anymore,
The things you want for me in life,
Get them later for your wife."

TALL SHADOWS, SMALL SHADOWS

The fire flamed upward
Tall shadows
Small shadows
Cast upon the misty grass
Slender, sturdy branches
Pierced through wieners
Mustard dripping
From the children's mouths
"Circle now, hold hands"
"You put your right foot in,
You take your right foot out,"
"Sing children."
Fading fires -
Shadows tall
Shadows small
No more shadows at all.

SUMMER VOICES

summer voices
about ringers
sling shots
fallen birds
pennants played
high jump
broad jump
pie contests
paper routes
birthday parties
sunday clothes
joyce's sister
teacher's pets
purple plums
wino bums
carnival prizes
tongue kisses
big butts
singers dancing
imagined romancing
boys talk
summer voices.

CHILDHOOD MEMORIES

We pitched our horseshoes in the summer breeze,
We rode our bikes on errands to the store,
We took some peaches from our neighbors' trees
But switched, we didn't do that anymore.

On Halloween, we went to trick or treat,
Our bags were filled with candy, nuts and fruit,
At Christmas time, we sang our carols sweet,
Expecting Santa in his big, red suit.

When cold set in, we taught ourselves to skate
On glassy beds of ice in the street,
Proud were we to learn the figure eight,
If we slipped, we got back on our feet.
Though times were hard, with many things to bear,
We survived, and learned to love and care.

8

LOVE AFTER WORLD WAR II
(Dedicated to Alma Hatchett of Turrell, Arkansas)

Through the halls we sauntered arm-in-arm,
With you in straight skirts and bobby socks;
I walked you to your class, then dashed to mine.

After school, we rocked on an enclosed porch,
Listening to Bull Moose Jackson on your box;
Survived the joys and fears of first mating.

In formal dress, we danced at our senior prom,
Our lips were softly sealed as "Stardust" played;
Put up our age to get in the Flame Show Bar.

Oh, I recall how thrilling was it all;
But I can hear the whistle of the train
That took you from my arms and out of my life.

Whenever I get sad and somewhat blue,
I rejoice in our wondrous love after World War II.

1986

NATURE CALLING

THE ROBIN'S SONG

At noon I heard a Robin sing,
Perched in a tree above,
A song that told my heart it's Spring,
A perfect time for love.

LOVE CALLING

Who's that knocking at my door?
It's quite a sound, you see,
A voice that I've not heard before,
Can it be love that's calling me?

TRANSITIONS

Now the summer days are gone
With their ample robes of splendour;
Fall has come upon us,
Wrapped in chilly winds and rain.
Winter menaces ahead,
Lord have mercy on us all.
Spring will cheer us up,
But will not last always.

11-6-92

BUTTERFLIES

All night long I lie awake in bed,
Making pretty poems in my head;
Remember them, when I try, at day,
Like butterflies, all have flown away.

June 1986

MORNING

Morning is more than light alone,
But a time for a new attitude
To be born,
A blessing for our precious lives.

Morning is the reality
That life is dear and with us yet,
Phenomenon we shouldn't forget -
We are not forsaken.

A blooming, morning is,
A blessing tenfold,
A happy, new beginning
Or a chance for renewal.

Fortunate, the one
To witness the rising sun,
For though our days are numbered,
Each morning is a gift from God.

Revised 4-12-93

WHAT KIND OF WIND ARE YOU?

Temperamental can be the winds
Or faithful, like old friends,
So what kind of wind are you?

Winds can do terrible things,
Like tornadoes and hurricanes
Or they can be gentle and warm
Like love after a storm,
So what kind of wind are you?

Winds can cut capers
So playfully, but like vapors,
Disappear as fast as they came;
They can be furious or tame,
So what kind of wind are you?

Seems the world gets windier each day,
Blowing every kind of way,
So what kind of wind are you?

WITH LOVING TOUCHES

FOR SANDRA: ONE RED ROSE
(To Sandra Redmond Woods on your Birthday, December 16, 1986)

A rose of red I give to you
The lifeline of my soul,
An expression of love and affection -
This one rose,
A reflection of yourself,
Singular in beauty,
Stellar in grandeur,
Strong in commitment.
I love you for yourself,
Just as you are,
As God made you,
Not as I would have you be.
Perfect no one is on earth,
But it is the way you strive to please,
With no deceit in your heart;
The love you give is so rare
For its genuine wholeness.
Your eyes are not without their tears,
But when I kiss them away,
You are peaceful and loving again,
Like the winds after the storm.
I love you mightily;
And please remember always,
This rose of red shall never fade
Away...

December 16, 1986

A SWEETER TRUTH: VALENTINE'S DAY 1985

I do appreciate, my love,
The pretty card that bears your name-
And of the box of chocolates,
You know I feel the same.
But on this special day, how great,
For us to find a sweeter truth,
If once again we re-create,
The passions of our youth.

PROMISES

We must make promises,
I know -
But promises to me
Have the taste
Of artichokes and asparagus,
Not forceful,
Like collard greens.

I like things to be strong,
Dependable,
Like John Coltrane's horn,
Or bountiful,
Like Aretha Franklin's voice.

If I had a choice,
I'd abolish promises
In favor of something else;
Something like
Fulfillment.

1984

WHAT IF...

If you had diamonds and fame,
Would you love me just the same?

If you had servants on call,
Would you love me at all?

If you had silver and gold,
Would you love me when I'm old?

If your answer is "No,"
Please pack your bags and go.

November 1985

WITH THIS RING

With this ring,
I thee wed,
In hopes that you will always sleep
At home in our own bed.

BEFORE YOU
(A Love Poem from the Sixties)

Before you
I existed,
Now,
I live;
Tomorrow,
We conquer.

June 2, 1983

LOVE

Once I was happy and smiled broadly,
Love was my companion.

Love is a kind of nice insanity,
One laughs walking down the street.

Love is not blind,
It sees stars and rainbows.

Love makes mountains seem not so high,
Easy to climb.

Love makes streams easy to ford,
Fortresses, not so impregnable.

Love is a vital force in the universe,
Staggering in the powers it commands.

But once love goes away,
The world gets cold and gray.

Icicles form around the soul;
One stares through a foggy windowpane.

I will travel mountains to the stars
If love would only pass this way again.

1987

LOVER

You are my pillow of dreams,
A concerto of moonbeams
And a symphony of ecstasy;
I love to kiss,
Your big, red, juicy lips.

12-4-84

PROMISED LAND

Toward a Promised Land we walk
Where streets are lined with gold and pearls;
Where chocolate-legged girls
With cinnamon eyes,
Strut with their braided heads held high
With just enough pride,
And love for the guys
As at Benin or Timbuktu.
You like to tease,
But your kisses are as sweet
As a spring breeze,
And those hips, which stick out
Nicely,
Are accented songs of syncopated joy.
Defrocked of silk and lace,
With a smile upon your face,
Your love for the men
Is the last citadel
of passions great reward.

January 1985

26

WE ARE THE NEWLYWEDS

I love my lady, across town
And my lady loves me,
But we could never married be
For that the Law would disallow

No bride for her
For me, no groom -
So I went to a hardware store
And we both jumped across a broom

Just like our forebears did in slavery -
But in Freedom, guess what?
I am married to her
And she is married to me

We are the newlyweds.

June 23, 1983

THIS JEWEL SIPPING SWEET RUM

where is her heart,
herself,
this jewel sipping sweet rum
when darkness
falls,
where are her lips
when love
calls
this jewel sipping sweet rum?

what should
we say
a working woman
in the day
fresh and bright,
but a tigress in the night?
where is her heart,
herself,
this jewel sipping sweet rum?

majestic and athletic,
lithe and lovely,
with her traces
of rum
she explodes;
yet within the deep abodes
of inner self
she queries life and love.

at night
she speaks with her body,
at nine
she speaks
with her mind.

it is another day,
traces of rum
have all gone away
and the nighttime
is banished.

May 23, 1981

TWO IN ONE

There are days
In which you are enraged,
Screaming at everyone
At the top of your lungs-
We get out of your way.

Then there are days
When peace pervades your heart-
There isn't anything
You wouldn't do
For anyone,
Smiling as you come to bed.
Two in one.

January 24, 1987

PRISONER IN YOUR ARMS

My lovely one,
Do not let me kiss and run,
Too soon, the sinking Sun
Disappears. Hold me, kiss me,
Squeeze me, and bind me
To your inner self.
Let me up only to turn Miles Davis over,
And to refreshen our glasses.
I like the way you say
"Hurry back to bed,"
That I've been gone way too long,
(Though it was just for a moment.)
Hold me, squeeze me, kiss me,
Bind me to your inner self,
I want no freedom from your satisfying charms,
Much too soon the Sun will reappear;
Make of me a prisoner in your arms.

1985

NO NEED FOR BITTER MEMORIES FROM THE PAST

After a while
Things become confused,

The more life you live,
More the dues.

Once a smiling face,
A gentle flower,
Much too soon
A warm embrace turns sour.

Love may not always last,
But there is no need
For bitter memories from the past.

Memorial Day 1983

A POEM FOR MOTHER LILLIAN REDMOND DIXON

In Spring
There is a special day
To honor Mothers
In a special way,
So Moms are showered
With cards and flowers
For all the hours
Of Mother's Day.
But for you,
Dear Lillian,
A Mother, tried and true,
Just one day
In every year
Is not enough for you;
So let your sons and daughters say,
What we have often said before,
Every day of every year
We love you more and more.
Happy Mother's Day.

May 9, 1982

For Sandra, Billy, James, Mimi, Tee, Arlene, Stella
and for the grandchildren & great-grandchildren

POEM FOR HATCHETT'S BABY
(A poem celebrating the birth of Alexis Hatchett)

What pleasures greet a mother new,
Caressing baby in her arms,
What infinite joy for Pappa, too,
A slave he'll be to all her charms;
The greatest prize in all the world,
And that's the way she'll stay,
A wise and healthy Hatchett girl,
Born this lovely Saturday.

4/15/78

SHIPWRECKED

I'm shipwrecked,
As blue as I can be -
My lover left me stranded,
In the middle of the sea.

I'm sending out this S.O.S.
Wherever you may be,
If you have a heart at all
Come and rescue me;

I'm shipwrecked.

January 31, 1985

CHICAGO WEEKEND

I long to have a weekend filled with fun,
In my hometown, things are rather slow;
I want to board a plane whose engines run
With wings pointed toward Chicago.

From the air, I see the skyline great
And I am thrilled to land at grand O'Hare,
Someone special greets me at the gate
Whose arms and lips tell me that they care.

As soon as I can put my baggage down,
We hail a cab and head for Chinatown;
On the menu, shrimp egg foo yong
With Chinese tea so soothing to the tongue.

On our way to a downtown movie show,
We view the towering sculpture by Picasso;
At the art museum, I buy some books
Of poetry by laureate Gwendolyn Brooks.

The "EL" train we ride out South tonight
To see if things have changed since Richard Wright;
Across the breadth of the town, we roam
Hoping Herbie Hancock has come home.

While I'm here I rid myself of cares,
Off to Soldier Field to see the Bears;
Peyton rambles on the Midway,
Breaking records on this windy day.

Oh, Chicago, must I leave so soon?
The magic of it all thrills me so -
But I'll be back some sunny afternoon,
So shed no tears for me as I go.

1985

THE JAZZ IN US

TOWARD A DANCE HALL WE GO

Toward a dance hall we go,
Where folks wear gold and cultured pearls
And chocolate-legged girls
With dark, hypnotic eyes
Smile and wink at the guys.

You like to tease,
But your kisses are as sweet
As a spring breeze
And those grooving hips
Matching movements of the beat
Are something wondrous to behold
Since they were made in Africa.

Rhythm queen, dance with me,
Make my night,
And when low goes the light,
I'm going to hold you
As close as I can.
We will both shut our eyes
And dance ever so close,
Until we leave this dance hall
Walking arm-in-arm.

WALTZING IN THE SNOW

(A Song for Dan Turner)

Dan was stylish going to school,
Mrs. Turner saw to that,
With his knickers and woolen sweaters -
But the rough boys didn't mess with Dan
Because they thought he was odd,
Sauntering home with his saxophone.
Once in the midst of winter-time,
Dan waltzed in the snow
His three-four tracks imprinted there.
Passing his house in the evenings
You could hear Dan's saxophone
With alacrity hitting sharps and flats.

Dan lost his Dad,
So down the long railroad track
He went, playing his somber horn;
Dan hit the road with groups
Whose names are lost to history,
Until he scored with the Ray Charles band,
For many years they loved his sound;
And with the fast-stepping Temptations
He traveled on the road -
Dan loved to play the Honky Tonk
Swinging his horn from side-to-side
And sometimes his sound was soft and warm.

Once when Dan came off the road
It seemed that he was so happy
Leaving the gig arm-in-arm
With this big-legged woman,
But who can trust the long road?
The horn grew weary,
And so did Dan.
"Don't wake me early, momma"
Dan called back to Mrs. Turner;
That was the night he slept away.
Had it not been for Dan's recorded saxophone
Mrs. Turner would have lived in that big house,
Alone.

November 10, 1992

ELVIN JONES

To the House of Jazz the figures go
Walking on the stage to start the show;
The leader joshes lightly with his men,
Then taps his toe, the signal to begin.

Notes of fluid beauty fill the air,
The faces of the patrons upturned now;
The leader adds his spices here and there
With sweat cascading down his heavy brow.

Oh, drummer, with your polyrhythmic fire
Forged in the cauldron of desire,
Some great ancestral gift, your drum roll,
Music from the heart that heals the soul.

The sets that have been played are history past,
His darling calls to him, "Please come on,"
The remnants of the fans are gone at last
As he and Keiko walk into the dawn.

October 1985

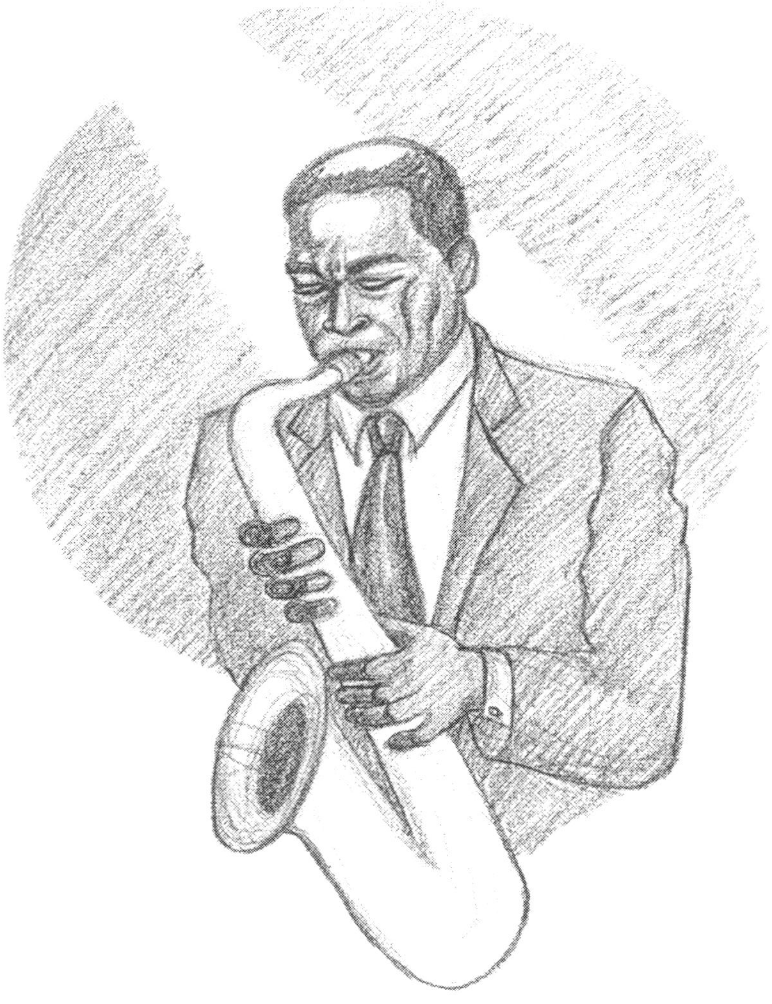

I SAW JOHN

John saw a New Jerusalem,
John, tall, dark and muscular
John, with a horn in his big hands
John, with a song in his heart
John, with life in his blood
John, with Elvin Jones on drums
John, with McCoy Tyner on piano
John, with Jimmie Garrison on bass
John, with the ability to captivate
John, I saw John,
John saw a New Jerusalem,
John, I saw John Coltrane.

Memorial Day 1983

SPRING

I know, I suppose,
Why Spring thrills me,
Why it is a mystery
In its warm sensuality,
Like the unheralded
Entrance of greenery,
Like birds that take off
In a singing spree,
Like love that comes
To you and to me
Naturally.

I love Spring
When daffodils dance on the hills
To Jazz,
And Lilacs form in their sassy bloom
Crowd the Garden Ballroom -
Gardenias kiss the gentle air
Just to let us know they're there
Lovely as ever, but blooming
For Billie Holiday.

I love Spring -
Spring is soft warmth
An auspicious beginning;
Rhythmic, like Chaka Khan
Don't you know,
Steady, like Al Jarreau -
Birds encamped on the hills
Prefer to sing like Stephanie Mills;
Then on special spring days
They try to sound like Maze.

Spring has brought us green,
Spring has brought us rain,
Spring has brought us everything,
Spring has brought us love.

June 8, 1983

JAZZ LOVERS

We got our spurs
On 52nd Street.
I held your hand
At Birdland,
Where pee wee M.C. Frankie Marquette
With his coat down to his knee,
Came on, saying,
"Ladies and Gentlemen,
Welcome to Birdland,
The Jazz capital of the world,
Please help me welcome,
Dizzy Gillespie and his big band."
"Manteca-"
And there we sat close together
While Bud Powell spun dreams
Of Polka Dots and Moonbeams.
Then we kissed in Chicago Town
To the ballads of Clifford Brown -
"What's New-"
A lilting alto sound we heard
Played by Yardbird
But he wasn't wearing
His Little Suede Shoes,
Only heavy dues.
We saw Horace Silver's
Straight, black hair
Drift into the piano keys
At Baker's in Detroit
Where he turned it out,
Thinking of his Dad, no doubt -
Seeing that we were Jazz lovers
Silver shook our hands after the set,
And then the musicians packed up and left.
After hearing all this soul,
Then came Rock and Roll.

                    December 16, 1984

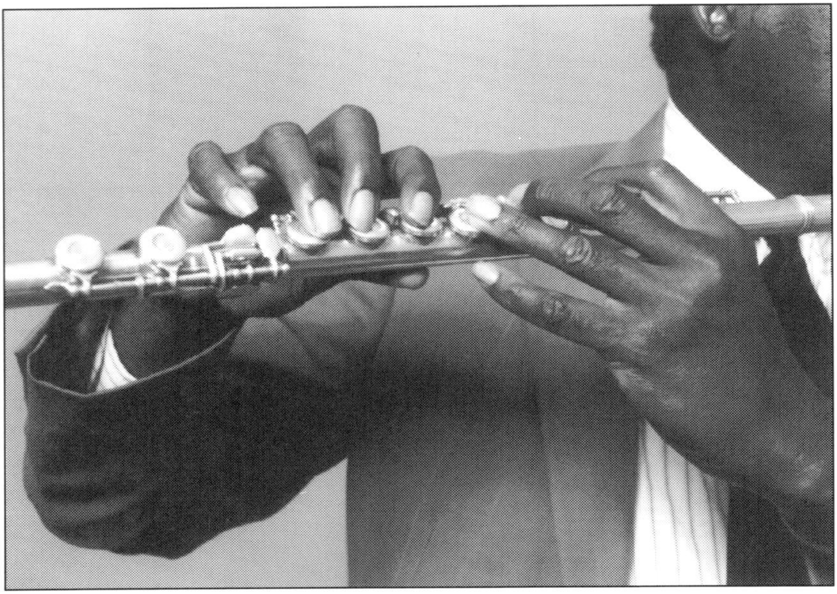

THE MUSIC OF THE FOUR SEASONS

The four seasons mean to me
Songs written in a different key.

Spring brings such pretty things,
It is a time to watch nature unfold:
Birds and flowers and warmth in the air,
Trees budding and grass springing up;
It is a time to plant the seeds of hope
To watch them grow in the garden of love.

In Summer, the earth heats up,
Children's voices are in the air;
I saw a child fall off her bike
But before I could get there to help out,
She dusted herself off and was on her way;
It's time to get the fishing rod or go for a dip.

Fall is so refreshing -
Apple cider and football games;
Even when birds begin to fly South
It is a time to be thankful;
Not hot like Summer, or cold like Winter,
Fall strikes a happy middle ground.

Snow can fall so softly in Winter,
Winds may whistle a song in your ears,
So dress warmly and don't catch a cold.
See if an elderly neighbor
Needs an errand run.
At Christmas, if you think of others
Someone will surely think of you.

The four seasons mean to me
Songs written in a different key.

JAZZ

On those short-sleeve summer nights
Bright marquee with flashing lights,
Dizzy, Miles, Monk, and Bird,
A brilliant brand of Jazz we heard.

Now in ripened years, we revel
Playing songs we love so well,
From an age too great to mourn
When classics of our own were born.

1987

SONGS FROM THE STORMY SKY

PART I - Tribute to Trane

I hear the distant thunderclap
And now the falling rain;
I hear in the winds of the storm,
A song by John Coltrane.

PART II - Tributes from the Living

Among the lightning and thunder,
Songs by McCoy and Elvin Jones,
Tributes to Trane and Garrison,
Sitting on their thrones.

February 3, 1986

BLUES OOZE INTO THE MIDNIGHT AIR

To Her Majesty's arms I will fly,
Heal my blues, by the blues,
My week-end road leads me
Straight to Chicago,
The Friday evening shadows will fall on me
In Chicago,
Where all of my provincial fears
                  Disappear.
I will not be bound by boredom's friendless grasp;
I will go to a midnight show,
Pop my fingers in a swinging joint,
And laugh as the wind from the Windy City
Blows my lady's dress up -
The sail boats stand at attention
On Lake Shore Drive,
As we head for the sassy southside,
I savor with my lips, Lem's barbecue,
My napkin softly wipes my fingertips
As week-end blues on 75th Street
75th Street blues, ooze
Ooze into the midnight air.

REMEMBERING MONK AND "RUBY, MY DEAR"

"Come in...
I've wondered where you have been
So long,
There's a song
I'd like you to hear,
Called 'Ruby my dear,'
By Thelonious Monk."

SOCIAL COMMENTS

PAPPA'S DREAM
(Remembering Rev. Joseph Shelby Woods)

A tall man took to the backyard mound,
beneath a beaming summer sky,
got his sign, then wound up
and let the pitches fly.

Some hit the heart of the plate,
some missed the mark, as in life,
but the youthful rhythms of this man,
thrilled his sons and wife.

Asleep, now, in that overstuffed chair,
no match for heat and fatigue,
dreaming of how great to have pitched
in the old Negro National League.

Pappa taught, though times may be hard,
Hone those dreams in your own backyard.

May 22, 1987

HEAR THAT LONESOME TRAIN WHISTLE

Hear that lonesome train whistle
Blowin' in the night,
Wheels of steel churning North,
Hands to work assembly lines,
Love and hate left behind;
Times were good, times were bad,
Now the lines are long,
The faces sad;
Things are made in Japan,
Taiwan, Korea, Mexico.
Hands and hearts grow tired;
Hear the lonesome train whistle
Blowin' in the night,
Wheels of steel headed South,
Headed way back home.

January 1987

INHERITANCE

So precious little material things
Our forebears left behind,
No stocks and bonds, but love and faith
Did their heirs find.

But for us, the offspring
Before we go to dust,
Some currency we'll also leave
That reads, "In God We Trust."

February 3, 1985

RUDE AWAKENING

Driving homeward
On a real bright summer day,
Happy and smiling,
My mind saw a great, big idea -
So exquisite
In its bold, shapely form
Until distracted,
I bumped hard into a car
In front of me
Parked at the light:
Shocked and shattered I thought,
That's enough for bright ideas today
Before they take my license away,
I just bumped into reality.

June 10, 1983

THE SALE OF A SOUTHERN FARM

They sit at bars with bets and boasts
Sporting mink and beaver skin,
Buying drinks and saying toasts
To those with glasses filled with gin.

Once at home, the headache's great,
But what the hell, no harm!
Though they have spent from the family estate
The funds from the sale of a southern farm.

                11/11/92

ELECTRONIC SALVATION

If you would have great blessings flow your way,
Don't wait, don't hesitate,
Send your money in this very day:
Ten, fifty, or hundred dollar bills,
And don't forget to leave us in your wills;
The more green you send to this address
The greater your chance of happiness,
So don't wait, don't hesitate,
If you would have great blessing flow your way,
Send your money in today,
Don't wait, don't hesitate,
Send your money right away.

11/11/92

THE SWEETEST FACES ON THE EARTH

The place where we were born,
The inner city,
Now is old and worn
And what a pity.

It could have been a great showplace,
If only we had will,
Where women strut in silk and lace
And men are dressed to kill.

Many moved to safer places
From the site of birth,
Away from inner city faces,
The sweetest on the earth.

1985

STARS IN HEAVEN STAY IN SHAPE

On Heaven's North end
The athletes with the darkened skin
Work out in their training camp,
Flexing their American muscles.

Here we find the Brown Bomber;
Mighty is he in Heaven
As he was on earth,
A hero bigger than life itself;
All the former strife
He knew, like Detroit
Poverty,
Made him stronger,
Not weak,
A symbol to all youth
To seek the truth,
To rise above adversity.

Heaven has no fighting
In its sphere,
But Louis will not waste time here,
So he finds strong
Jack Johnson
And they shadow box,
Fainting, moving,
With the left foot
Always out front -
They slip each others lightened punches
And have fun
In Heaven's Sun,
As two more heavyweights
Who also passed
Through Heaven's gates,

Ezzard Charles
And big Sonny Liston,
Square off -
Like Jack and Joe
They do not pass
A heavy blow
Which would Heaven
Displease;
Indeed,
Both in their own
Way
And in another
Day,
Heaven knows
Threw plenty blows
On Earth.

On a diamond to the North
Satchel Paige,
A pitching great
Of his own age,
Throws from Heaven's Mound
Balls to a fellow
Named Roy Campanella,
Who no more
Needs an old
Wheelchair;

Up to the plate
Steps another great
Holding high his bat
Waiting for the pitch,
But hits two foul tips -

Then he gets his fast ball
Which he drives o'er
Heaven's wall -
The cheering has begun
For Jackie Robinson
And for his acclaim
Someone says he made
The Baseball Hall of Fame;
As he rounds Heaven's bases
Jackie winks at Branch Rickey.

On a temporary track,
Paved on Heaven's
Street of gold,
A figure fleet of feet
Sees if his form
He can get back,
So he works high hurdles
And tries the long
Broad jump,
The muscles in his
Legs so prominent
As they were
In Germany;
Jesse Owens
Works alone
In his new
Home,
But now and then
He misses
The southside
Of Chicago.

So he gives a smile
As he makes another record
For the quarter mile,
And for his blinding
Speed
An angel places
Gold around his neck.

On another track,
Heaven's spectators
View with great delight
Two Black jockeys
Riding fast white horses
To the Finish line:
Murphy muses in Heaven
How he captured the Kentucky Derby,
Riding high on earth
As throngs cheer him
Crossing the bar
First,
So he doffs his cap
To the crowd
And waves with his crop.
All in all these figures great
Keep on staying in shape,
Though they have all passed
Through Heaven's beauteous gate.

SCREAM OUT LOUD

My doctor says I'm getting much too plump,
That I must drop some pounds from thighs and rump.

Fried foods, the doctor says to halt
And from the table, take away the salt.

While I ponder better things to eat,
The dentist dares to pull the tooth that's sweet.

The spirits I imbibe, Doc says renounce;
I take my cup and pour out every ounce.

The smoking habit, doctor says forget;
I take my foot and crush the cigarette.

The doctor says that I should learn to hike;
With chagrin, I pull out my old bike.

He says that I should buy one built for two;
A flame in my heart will help me through.

On my return, he says I should be proud;
I feel so good that I could scream out loud.

Summer 1985

POEM TO THE GRANDMOTHER I NEVER SAW

I never saw you
Grandma,
But I heard talk
Of the strength you packed
On a small frame,
The hills climbed
In the Blue Grass State -
How you fed many
With so little
After Grandpa died;
One of those was momma
Who left you at 15
To get married.
She moved away,
Taking with her
A part of you,
Your toughness on
A small frame
And the ability
To care for so many
With such little.
So I salute
You, my grandma
How much I do
Respect
The wise
In each strand
Of your gray hair
And although
My eyes
Never saw yours,
How much talk I heard of you,
Grandma,
How well I feel I know you
Grandma,
How much strength
You packed on a small
Frame.
        11-11-92

THE LITERARY FIGURES

OF PRESIDENT CHARLES SPURGEON JOHNSON

Receding hairline, then,
Charles Spurgeon Johnson,
The first Black president,
Strolling across the Fisk Campus
Like a refined lion
In a double-breasted suit,
Ready for the attack;
Strides in your walk
For your people
And a disciplined mind.

Your work still stands
Undisturbed by time,
A great compliment.
Too soon you left us
In what was your bloom.
But we know your shining legacy,
A bevy of searching minds,
Mentally brave young men and women,
Who later became
Scientists and scholars
Physicians and poets
Teachers and preachers
Who learned your lesson well:
Search for truth.
So God be ever with you,
Charles Spurgeon Johnson,
And may you always rest in peace.

ARNA BONTEMPTS

To the campus post-office
He made his trek,
With a smile on his face
For his students,

Or he sat in the Fisk Chapel
Listening to Mattawilda Dobbs:
Langston Hughes came down to see him
Like other Black bards.

But you would never have known
That fame smiled upon him
This white-haired Louisianian
The way he carried himself
Not appearing superior.

Bontempts gave to his students
More than books:
He gave a cheerful "Good Morning,"
He gave a teacher's encouragement
And a compliment for doing your best.
Now that he is laid to rest,
We know that he meant much more
Than the recommendations he wrote;
What mattered, the thoughts behind them.

And long after campus days had passed
Here comes this missive
From another city,
Inquiring about yourself and your family,
Saying in essence,
"Keep with it, things will work out."
These are the thoughts that linger
When we think of a teacher.
Thus was Arna Bontempts,
At a time when the stars and moon
Shown upon us in Nashville.

TO PAUL LAURENCE DUNBAR'S HOUSE WE GO

Pappa took me, in my youth,
To Dayton, Ohio, in search of truth,
In Paul Lawrence Dunbar's house we found,
Oak and Ivy, ready bound.

February 14, 1985

REMEMBERING ROBERT HAYDEN

He rambled through the musty, dusty stacks
at the Library, Erastus Milo Cravath,
thick lenses better to see the truth.

Emerged into the Nashville sunshine
books pressed against his searching breast,
armed to the tooth.

Spot slaveships ply their westward way,
repulsed by putridness and screaming slaves
who dared to jump into the jaws of sharks
than work the fingers to the bone, enchained.

A man accustomed to the hard truths,
child of the east side, Detroit's Black Bottom
where he said no roses grew in Summer -

Oh, how slow we are to crown the wise -
but Senegal refused to pass him by.

February 16, 1987

PURPLE RIVER
To Anne Russell

Soon I am going home
To see with my own eyes
The beauty and the pain of Africa;
To view, for myself,
The purple river
Anne Russell saw -
Flowing and weaving its way into eternity.

I see so well the river;
I feel the river, in myself,
And soon I will
Go
To Africa,
To see with mine own eyes,
The purple river
My friend
Anne Russell saw.

ROBERT HAYDEN, I DIDN'T KNOW WHO YOU WERE

Fame concealed you as long as she dared,
Robert Hayden; I didn't know who you were
On your way to your classes, books pressed
Against your lonely breast; thick glasses;
I didn't know who you were,
A simile or a metaphor
Glistening in the Nashville sun,
A silhouette against Jubilee Hall.
Out of the bowels of Detroit's Black Bottom,
"No roses there in Summer" you wrote.
Heard the jangling church tambourines,
Saw the pimps and painted prostitutes,
Emerged with a face of peace and pain,
Carrying no other weapon in the streets
Than a dynamite poem.
Robert Hayden, I didn't know who you were,
But with each passing year,
I get a chance to know you more and more.

January 28, 1987

A SALUTE TO NIKKI GIOVANNI

One finds no empty phrases
In her verse -
About our struggles and our troubles,
Vacillation has no home.

Nikki Giovanni,
By eastern Tennessee sunshine kissed;
Sights set so high
Like the Cumberlands, near Jellico.

Once touched by the muse,
Upon this soil you joined
That great tradition beginning, they say
With Lucy Terry and Phyllis Wheatley.

So, go ahead and poetize
Sister of destiny,
Help us all to realize
The inner wealth we own.

SOCIAL PROTEST

RUN, SLAVES, RUN

Old master bragged to everyone
His happy slaves would never run,
But long before the break of day,
The slaves ran away.

Run, slaves, run,
Never stop till victory's won -
Headed North to freedom's soil,
Nevermore as slaves to toil.

Lacerated backs were burning,
In their breasts, freedom yearning;
Master at the big house, scowling,
To the chase, dogs howling.

Run, slaves, run,
Run until freedom's won,
No more taste of slavery's sting,
Never going back again.

Freedom, freedom, oh, how sweet,
To slaves with bruised and swollen feet,
Safely reach a land so far,
Guided by the North Star.

A slave has got a big heart,
From the old plantation part;
A fugitive means to me,
A hero fresh from slavery.

Run by night, hide by day,
An underground along the way,
With folks who help feed your mouth,
For slaves escaping from the South.

Run, slaves, run,
Never stop till victory's won,
Headed North to freedom's soil,
Nevermore as slaves to toil,
Nevermore as slaves to toil.

June 1985

Du BOIS

The lion wore a bearded face,
warrior for a wounded race,
classic books to prove his case,
preached Pan-Africa, embrace.

Fisk and Harvard shaped his head,
Complained that Booker T. misled,
brought to trial, his heart bled,
died in Ghana, but not dead.

1986

THE LIFE AND DEATH OF A SLAVE

Work and work but nothing keep,
Till the soil but never reap,
Cry those weary eyes to sleep,
This is the life of a slave.

Pick that cotton, mend that fence,
Lashed for showing little sense,
Early home in an unmarked grave,
The life and death of a slave.

December 19, 1986

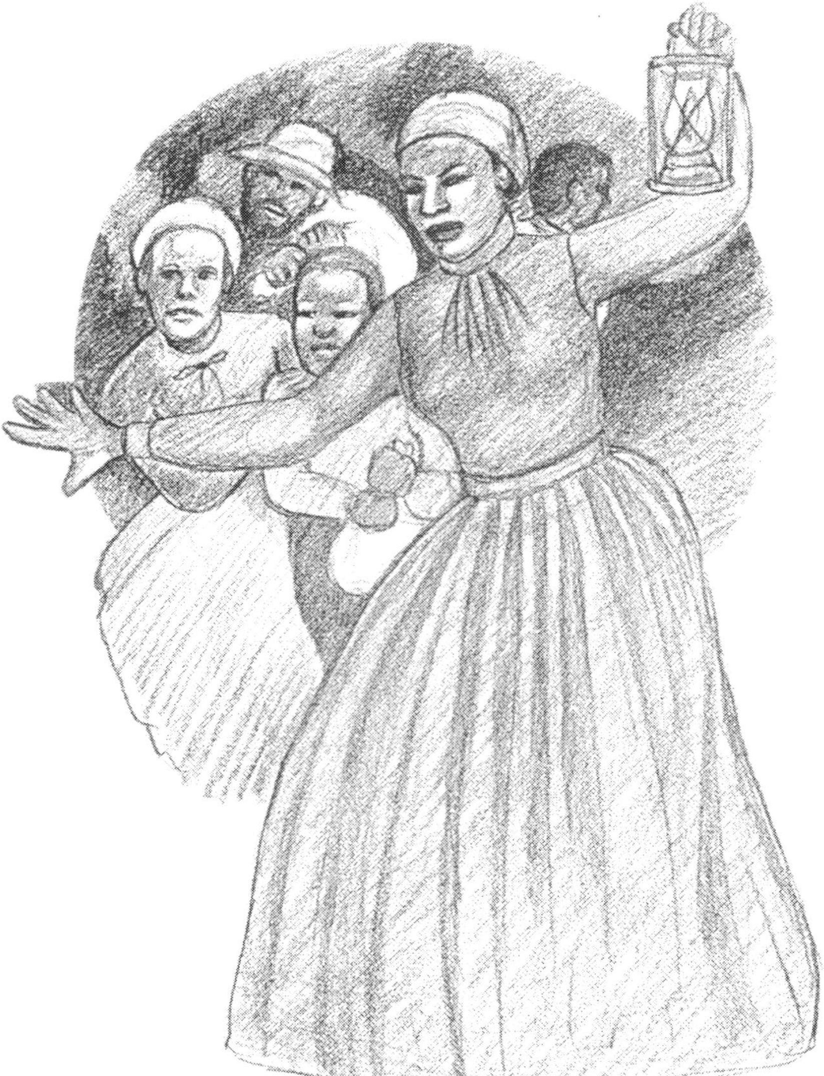

A WILY SLAVE WILL ALWAYS FIND A WAY

Can you imagine?
A slave walking all the way
From Down Home to Detroit?
To Canada, by boat, the easy part.
Does that tell us something?
A wily slave will always find a way.

1985

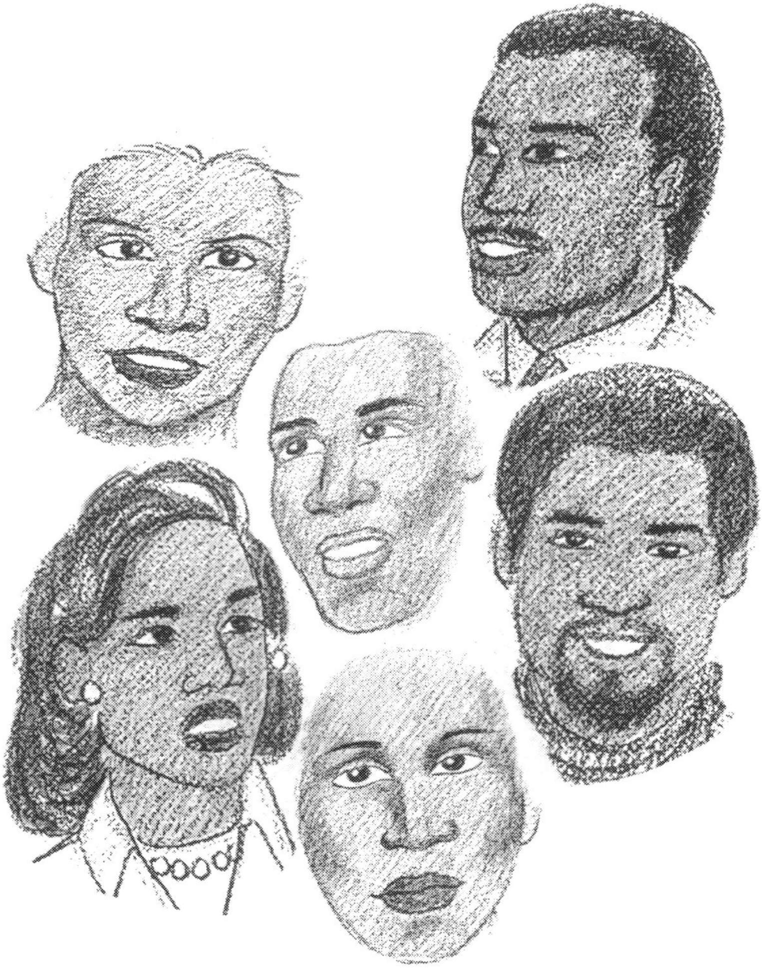

LEGACY OF LOVE

These dark, downtrodden hearts,
Removed to an unknown, western world,
Did not even own themselves,
Nor did they have the right to love,
Our Black forefathers and mothers:
But they loved one another, anyway,
Many times by stealth in night or day,
Through the hard, empty years,
And through the scars and tears;
They loved in spite of endless toil,
Though they tilled the thankless soil.
Masters saw but happy souls
Cast in simple roles;
But a slave's smile is quite a sight to see,
Ask Nat Turner and Denmark Vesey.
Chastised, they loved on,
Whipped, they loved their own,
Sold down the river, they cried,
And loved the memory of those,
Nevermore to see.
They left for you and me,
A touching legacy of love.

February 24, 1985

AT HEAVEN'S GOLDEN PODIUM

Garvey and Du Bois have not resolved,
The issue that to Africa return,
"Fine for you, but not so for the rest?"
Garvey chides the lion, half in jest -
The angels have to separate the two.
Booker T. gets into the act,
But reprimanded for the Atlanta address,
He says that he can point to much success,
Standing yet, Tuskegee Institute.
So on and on they go
As onlookers marvel at their eternal wit.
The three still cannot agree
At Heaven's golden podium,
On the issues too hot for this earth.

KING'S DREAM

Martin Luther King with his dream,
Had a preview of the Promised Land.
In this world, he does not hesitate,
To talk with Lincoln of their common fate,
As men like Gandhi listen by;
Those who freedom preach are felled too soon.
So early the peaceful ones
Go to Heaven violently.

"OUT"

A lasting mark in life
I hoped to make,
Strike the ball with power
Down the line,
But here comes this official
From his chair,
Just to look and call the ball
"Out."

April 1987

A POEM FOR TWO CHAMPIONS OF THE CAUSE
(In Honor of Attorney Milton Henry
and Attorney Elbert Hatchett)

So many dangers lurk along the path,
Where howling wolves at the crossroads wait,
To heap upon our souls their ceaseless wrath,
Against our faces slam the prison gate.

Champions of the cause we ever need,
Defenders of our precious liberty,
As Henry and Hatchett, who for justice plead,
That one day all of God's children will be free.

Henry came to us from the East,
Hatchett is our loyal native son,
Both have faced the dragon and the beast,
Dramatic victories have these warriors won.

For Hatchett has a lancet in his hand,
Henry, by his side, a shining sword,
Both have lucid minds at their command
And Henry adds to Law the Holy Word.

Oh, brothers, whom we dearly claim as ours,
How proud are we to honor you this way,
No accolades beneath the gleaming stars,
Great enough our thanks to you convey.
Though years go by, both of you be sure
The legend of your works will long endure.

June 1986

THIS LAND BELONGS TO ALL OF US

We must resist the dissipated dream
That leaves us frustrated and forlorn;
We seek to know who we are
And where we are going.

Brought here in shackles,
Freedom came at long last
With help and comfort here and there;
But now, where are we going, where?

No time to lick our wounds
Applied by history's sting,
The world still mocks
The ladder's last wrung.

"Go back home to stay,"
The ugly voices chant,
But should all go back home
Except the Native Americans?

We say the land belongs to all
To all who toiled upon the soil;
We say, work it out,
This land belongs to all of us.

FAITH AND HOPE

WORDS IN MY HEAD

Words are spinning
In my head,
Pearls of wisdom
From the dead -
Momma's words,
Pappa's words,
And things that other folks have said.
Once I thought myself to be,
Someone pretty well-read,
But I just keep on hearing
Words of wisdom in my head -
Warm words,
Soothing words,
And words of admonition,
Like, "Pray, son, Pray."
I sometimes wonder to myself,
If they have really gone away.
All are still alive to me,
Through words in my head.

January 15, 1985

NO ONE COMES TO MY HOUSE, ANYMORE

No one comes to my house, anymore,
Nobody rings the bell,
But there were throngs that came before,
When we were raising hell.

A visitor knocked at my door
And filled my heart with the spirit,
No one comes to my house, anymore
Because nobody wants to hear it.

November 1985

LORD, I'LL CONFESS

Lord, I'll confess –
You know that I have sinned
Lord,
I'll go to church and pray,
I'll bow my head, and ask you
Lord,
To wash my sins away.

Lord, I'll confess
You know I've done wrong
Lord,
But when I feel alone,
I'll place my heavy cares and woes
Lord,
Upon the Heavenly throne.

January 31, 1985

HEAR THOSE SHAKING TAMBOURINES

Hear those shaking tambourines
Late at night, late at night,
Syncopated hopes and sanctified dreams,
At the corner Church of God in Christ.

Sister on piano, chording,
Heavy beats the drummer playing,
Folks that speak in tongues are praying
At the Corner Church of God in Christ.

Oh, souls that dance the Holy dance,
Back and forth and side to side,
In the aisles, the spirits glide
At the corner Church of God in Christ.

Heavy beat, dancing feet,
Sounds that drift into the street,
Folks so filled with the Holy Ghost
At the corner Church of God in Christ.

Hear those shaking tambourines
Late at night, late at night,
Syncopated hopes and sanctified dreams
At the corner Church of God in Christ.

IN MEMORIUM

MY SISTER GROWS OLDER DAY BY DAY
(Dedicated to Manjolene Woods McCaskill)

My sister grows older
Day by day,
Little we can say
To soothe her aging heart.
In the morning, she is slow to start
Her daily activities -
Certain natural proclivities
To promptly begin work
Are lost; now she will shirk
A task; what was once no chore,
Washing dishes, hanging out the clothes,
Shopping at the store,
Now my sister loathes.
Her body aches and pains,
Nothing much of youth remains -
Yet, my sister never complains,
Or contemptuously rails at fate -
She accepts her declining state
Rather majestically, I think.
When I consider
The women who become bitter,
Lifeless and incurably sad,
Looking back to how life was,
I become glad
My sister gets on
As well as she does.

LINES TO A YOUNG HERO
(In memory of Leo Sharkey - Fisk University Fullback)

Young hero
Fleet-footed star
The season's past

The evening lines
Have moved across
The silent stadium

Cheers are hushed
Confetti fallen down
To the ground.

We stand aghast
Mute and dumb
God's dazed creatures.

Most of us
Can never run
One-hundred yards

The slippery sod
Much too soon
We fall upon

Young hero
We still recall
Your dashing sprints
The games won
When all odds
Foretold humiliation

The injured leg
On which you
Ran to victory

For Gold and Blue
The raving love
You bore within

But above all
We shall recall
Your pleasant personality

Young hero
Rest in peace
We shall remember.

TO MOTHER KAY, OUR DISTINGUISHED MEDAL OF HONOR
(In Memory of Mrs. Keola Hatchett)

When we were young, searching to find ourselves,
You opened the doors to your home, Mother Kay
To keep us kids off the streets.
Let us play our syncopated songs
On your living room piano,
In the background, you listened with your heart,
One who appreciated the works of Marian Anderson
And the haunting blues of Bessie Smith.
You brought up North, the best of southern traditions:
We admired the way you carried yourself,
Majestic, with your head held high,
Admired your passionate commitment to your family
And your dedicated warmth to all of us;
For this you win our distinguished Medal of Honor
And in that great gettin' up morning
When all the saints shall rise and rejoice forever,
We pray to see your pristine face, again.

March 14, 1987

THE FARM IN TENNESSEE
In Loving Memory of Grandma Albinda Redmond

In Williamson County, Tennessee,
An old gravel road takes over,
Winding its way up a hill
To a tall, unpainted house
With sagging, green shingles,
Fading photographs hanging
On walls with high ceilings,
Old Seth Thomases strike no more upon the hour;
Outdoors no water is in the duck pond,
No tobacco curing in the barn;
The outhouse leans precariously to the side.
Only aged people know
A lady named Albinda ran this farm -
She gave love to all of us,
The greatest gift of all Albinda gave
Then she returned to dust in her grave.

June 30, 1983

TO DEWALT
A MAN WITH A HEART OF GOLD

My friends,
Here comes Dewalt,
A well-dressed,
Citizen of the World -
A man with a
Scintillating mind
And a heart of gold.

In youth, at Pontiac
He was a dashing basketeer,
All-State he made
In a very good year
Then he basked in
    The Sun
       at Florida
Studying books.
There are other things we
    know -
He strolled the streets
    of Chicago
Shoulders tall and straight;
Harlem he knew after dark
As well as he knew Central Park.

In Washington, D.C.
He walked the
Halls of Ivy
Getting his Law degree.
Then his footsteps
    Headed home;
    We opened up our
    waiting arms

To all of his not-to-be
    forgotten charms.
He chased his daughter Stacy
    at Hatchett's Ranch
And heard her squeals of sheer
    delight.
Then he saw her off to bed
    at night,
Saying,
"Sleep well, apple of my eye."
The man knew life
The man knew joy,
And the man knew strife.

He danced in the moonlight
    of the city,
He rejoiced in its splendour
    and magnificence,
For he was a city man,
A citizen of the World
And a man with
    A heart of gold.
Heaven has opened up
Her spacious arms to him,
While Angels praise him
For his work on earth.

12-7-81

PLATO

I waited in the family line,
Took my turn,
Then I saw his face
Dead
At the parlour.
I waited in the family line,
Took my turn
Going out.
I waited in the family line
At the grave of dust:
I perched my elbows in a long blue car,
Then I cried and cried.

8-17-83

BETH

Beth will not be with us anymore,
Her ashes are all strewn in the West
Where the wind intercepts her gentle smile
And cheerfully returns it back to us.

Half a century of love, Beth knew
And still she holds the hand of her loving man;
So kind was she, so warm and understanding;
Though absent, she will ever present be.

In her world there are no sleepless nights
Or any days of bitter memories;
The pain is for those who remain; husband and friends
Who recall the beauty of this woman and weep.
Though time goes by, the lustre of her life
Will not fade away or diminish in worth.

December 21, 1987

Thunder and Lightning is the second book written by Esmo Woods. His first book, called *Pontiac: The Making of a United States Automobile Capital - 1818-1950,* was published in 1991. The book has brought numerous honors, awards and citations to its author including citations from the U.S. House of Representatives and from the U.S. Senate. Distinguished American historian, Dr. John Hope Franklin, James B. Duke Professor of History Emeritus at Duke University wrote of Woods' book, "It is a perfect model for writing of the whole history of a community." Dr. Charles H. Wright, the physician who founded the Museum of African American History in Detroit, commended Woods on his history book and added, "If we could get writers in other cities to follow your example, we would all be better off." The book is approved for use by school districts in several states.